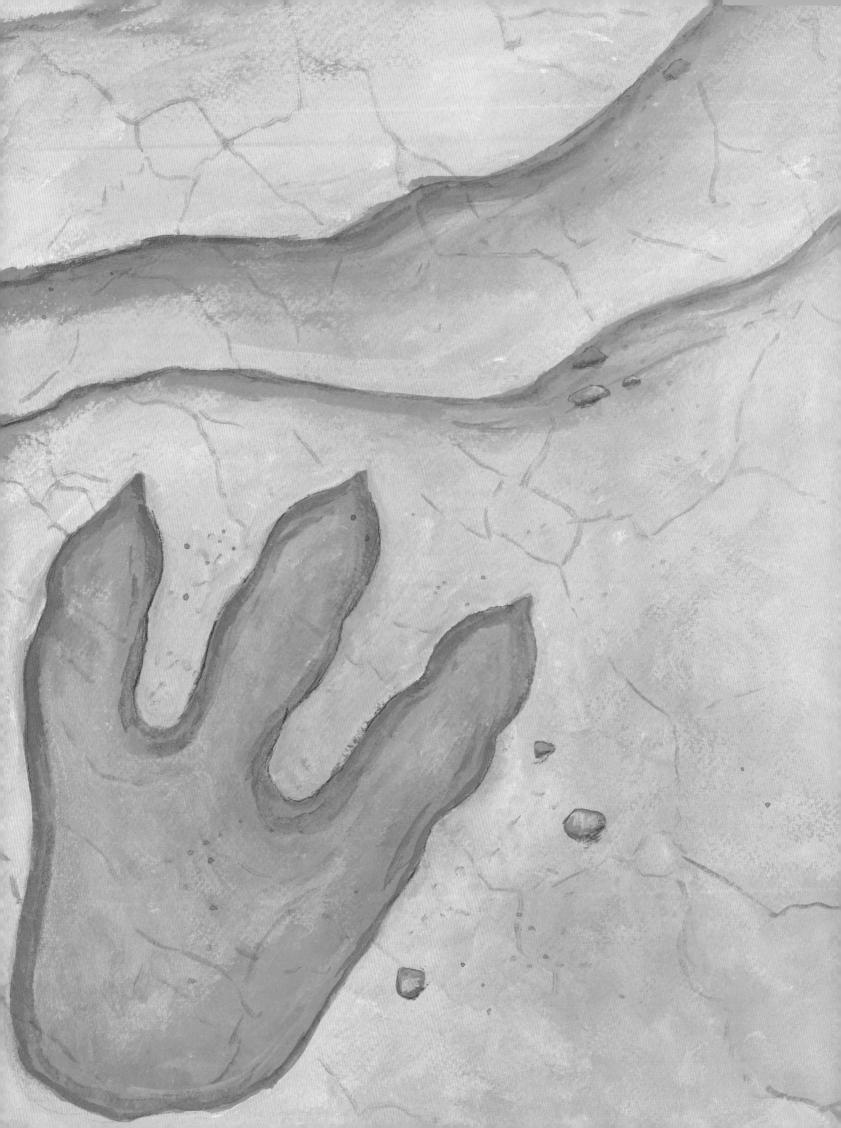

BARNUM BROWN
Dinosaur Hunter
DAVID SHELDON

Walker & Company

New York

On February 12, 1873, William and Clara Brown wanted to give their newborn son a special first name. Inspired by the famous showman P. T. Barnum, whose traveling circus happened to be in their town, Carbondale, Kansas, the Browns named their son Barnum. And true to his name, Barnum grew up to be an exceptional young man.

Every day after school, Barnum loved to go exploring. Millions of years in the past, the area around the Browns' farm had been a vast ocean. Barnum often found fossils of ancient sea creatures. But he always made it home in time for supper, usually carrying a new discovery.

After supper, the Browns would read the newspaper accounts of amazing new discoveries. The Great Dinosaur Rush of 1877 began when two dinosaur hunters, Edward Cope and Othniel Marsh, began a fierce rivalry, competing for dinosaur fossils in the American West. As a result, the lost world of dinosaurs was revealed like never before.

Barnum imagined what it might be like to explore for a seventy-foot-long *Apatosaurus*, come upon an armor plated *Stegosaurus*, or even be chased by a three-horned *Triceratops*! He just knew there had to be more amazing dinosaurs out there to discover.

Barnum's love of dinosaurs and exploring never left him. He went on to study dinosaurs (a subject called paleontology). Before long, he knew exactly what he wanted to do. He went to work for Henry F. Osborn, the director of the American Museum of Natural History, in New York City. The museum had bears, elk, sea turtles, herons, alligators, and countless other animal specimens and skeletons on display, but not one dinosaur. It would be Barnum's job to search for dinosaur fossils.

The best place to look for dinosaur fossils at the time was in the dry, forbidding "badlands" of the western United States and Canada. Beneath the clay and sandstone hills was a buried treasure of ancient animal bones. And that's where Barnum started searching.

In those days, before the automobile, the only way to get to a possible dinosaur site was by horse and wagon. The work could be hot, exhausting, and dangerous, but Barnum was determined to find something never seen before.

Before long, the American Museum of Natural History was receiving the extraordinary finds of Barnum Brown. Giant bones, protected in a burlap and plaster wrap (a method Barnum developed himself), arrived by the crateload.

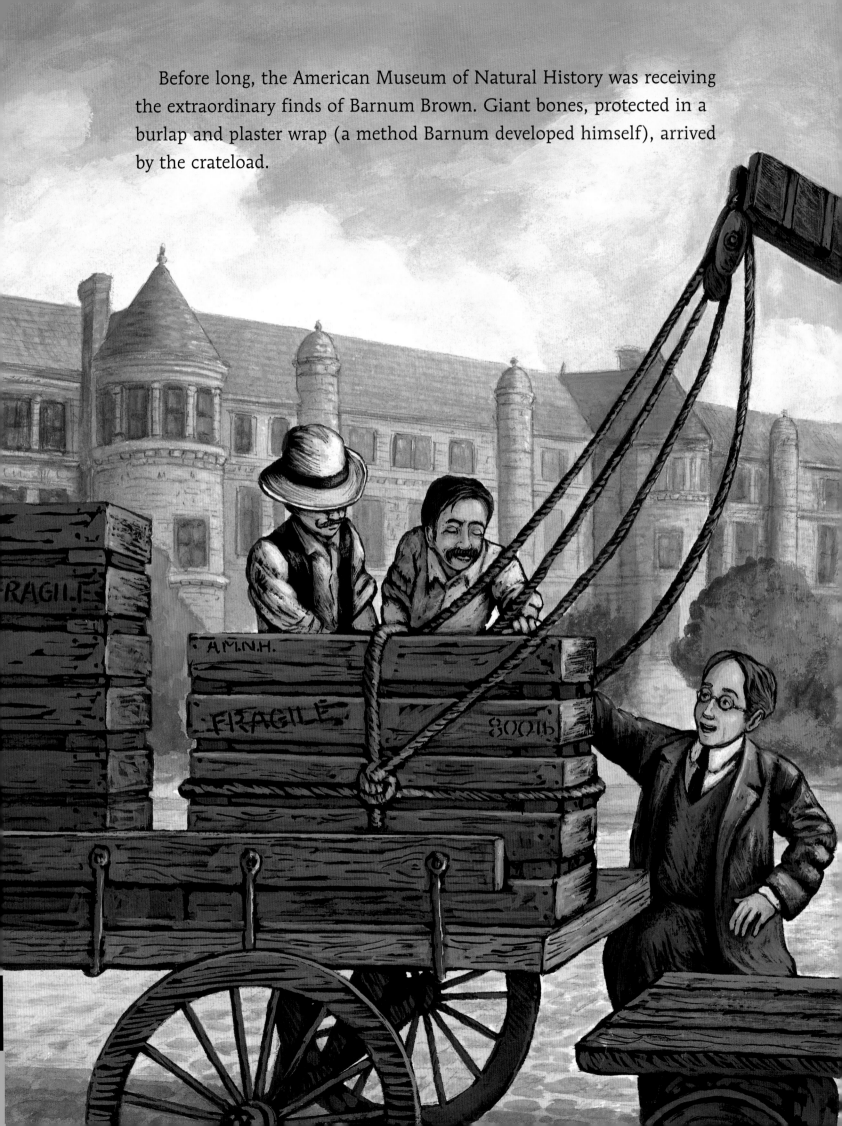

It was Henry Osborn's job to put together, describe, and name the new dinosaur discoveries. Other museums, such as the Carnegie Museum in Pittsburgh, had teams out searching for their own dinosaur fossils. Osborn dreamed about having the best collection of dinosaurs in the world, and he was counting on Barnum to help him realize his dream.

Barnum became so good at finding dinosaur fossils that Osborn would say he could smell the bones! Like his famous namesake, Barnum could be a real showman. Very often, he was found working merrily in a dusty dinosaur "quarry," carefully removing layers of clay and sandstone around a fossil while wearing a stylish hat, tie, and fur coat!

In 1898, Barnum's team of diggers began to uncover the first complete dinosaurs for the museum in Como Bluff, Wyoming, including an "old friend," a huge *Apatosaurus*. As he worked, Barnum imagined what a family of *Apatosaurs* might have looked like.

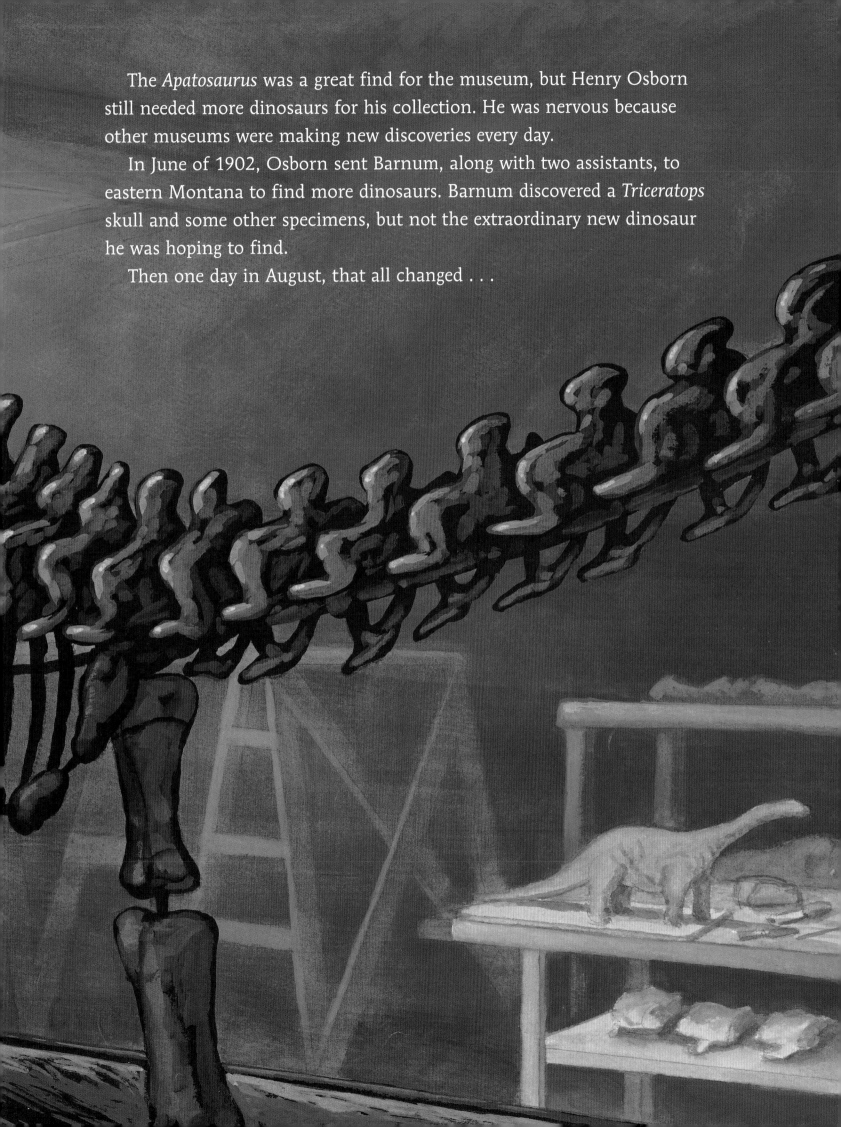

The *Apatosaurus* was a great find for the museum, but Henry Osborn still needed more dinosaurs for his collection. He was nervous because other museums were making new discoveries every day.

In June of 1902, Osborn sent Barnum, along with two assistants, to eastern Montana to find more dinosaurs. Barnum discovered a *Triceratops* skull and some other specimens, but not the extraordinary new dinosaur he was hoping to find.

Then one day in August, that all changed . . .

Barnum Brown was hot. As he wiped the sweat from his forehead, it awed him to think that this same sun may have shined down on some enormous dinosaur, millions of years in the past, whose bones were just waiting to be uncovered.

It had been a long day. Barnum was just about to give up looking any further, when something caught his eye.

Barnum knelt down and began to scrape away at the hard sandstone. Slowly, the telltale signs of a fossil began to emerge. Barnum's eyes widened. This was something he had never seen before. He called over his assistants, and together they set about the slow task of exposing the whole fossil.

Barnum was thrilled. Not only was this dinosaur a new discovery, but by the size of its teeth, it must have been a ferocious predator, the likes of which the modern world had never seen! It took two years to uncover all the pieces of this mystery dinosaur.

Back at the museum, Osborn and his staff assembled the pieces and were amazed by what they saw. Osborn named the new dinosaur *Tyrannosaurus Rex*, "Tyrant Lizard King." It had lived on the earth some sixty-five million years ago, surely spreading fear wherever it had roamed. Barnum discovered a second *T. Rex* in 1908, this one a nearly complete specimen.

When the final display was presented to the public, there were gasps throughout the hall. *T. Rex* was an overnight sensation, and Barnum Brown became known as the greatest of all dinosaur hunters!

Just two years after the discovery of the second *T. Rex*, Osborn sent Barnum to search the Red Deer River in the badlands of western Canada. Barnum designed a special flatboat to help his team explore the steep cliff walls for dinosaurs.

Not to be outdone in their own backyard, the Canadian government hired noted dinosaur hunter Charles H. Sternberg and his sons, George, Levi, and Charles Jr., to compete directly with Barnum's team. They constructed their own boat—and a new Dinosaur Rush was on!

The Sternbergs worked all day at their sites. It was difficult work, but the thrill of a new discovery kept them going. Just knowing Barnum Brown's team was digging nearby made them work even harder. The two groups enjoyed a friendly rivalry. But no one had a nose for finding dinosaurs like Barnum Brown.

Back at his quarry, Barnum and his team had another amazing find: *Saurolophus*. Emerging from the clay and sandstone were the fossilized remains of a creature that had not seen the light of day for seventy-five million years!

Because of their hard work and fierce competition, Barnum and the Sternbergs uncovered many important dinosaur fossils, including . . .

Saurolophus (saw-ROL-oh-fus)
Discovered by Brown's team, 1911.

Albertosaurus (el-ber-toh-SAWR-us)
First complete specimen discovered by
Brown's team, 1914.

Corythosaurus (co-RITH-oh-SAWR-us)
Discovered by Brown's team, 1912.

Styracosaurus (sty-RAK-o-SAWR-us)
Discovered by Brown's team, 1915.

Edmontonia (ed-mon-TO-ne-ah)
Discovered by the Sternbergs, 1917.

Hailed as the Second Great Dinosaur Rush, Barnum Brown's competition with the Sternbergs helped create one of the world's richest collections of dinosaurs. Osborn's dream had become a reality. Barnum Brown worked for the American Museum of Natural History for sixty-six years, eventually becoming Head Curator of Paleontology. After he retired, Barnum continued to give tours of his beloved dinosaurs, affectionately calling them his "children."

Digging Further into the Story

The first mounted dinosaur fossil put on display in the United States was a standing *Hadrosaur* skeleton constructed by Waterhouse Hawkins in 1868 for the Academy of Natural Sciences in Philadelphia. The public response was so overwhelming that a great rush began to find new dinosaur fossils.

Edward Cope, a paleontologist working for the academy, set out to find new dinosaurs in the American West. At the same time, Othniel Marsh from the Yale Peabody Museum put together his own team of dinosaur hunters and began searching the same area. At first, the two men were friendly, but as the competition for fossils became more intense, their friendship disintegrated. Both men sent teams (sometimes armed) to muscle out the other from new dinosaur sites. And when either man was finished with a site, he would have his men destroy any remaining fossils to keep them from his rival. Their feud even went on in the newspapers and scientific journals. Marsh publicly humiliated Cope by pointing out that Cope had mistakenly placed the head of a *Plesiosaur* on its tail rather than its neck! Yet their research helped establish western America as a prime dinosaur fossil location.

By the end of the nineteenth century, when Barnum Brown began his search, the study of dinosaurs had become an established and respected science. Barnum first discovered the lower jawbone and neck bones of *Tyrannosaurus Rex* (*T. Rex*) on an expedition in 1900, while searching for a *Triceratops* skull. Still searching for *Triceratops* fossils in 1902, he discovered the first nearly complete *T. Rex* skeleton along the steep bluffs of Hell Creek in eastern Montana. Returning to the same area in 1908, Barnum spied some vertebrae along a cliff wall that turned out to be one of the most complete *T. Rex* skeletons ever found. The original museum display aimed to have both *T. Rex* specimens included in a dramatic fighting scene. In the end, only one could be displayed because the museum simply didn't have enough room for both!

The original display of *T. Rex* had it standing upright with its tail dragging along on the ground. But further scientific research over the years revealed dinosaurs walked more like birds with their tails in the air to counterbalance all the weight up front. Barnum's *T. Rex* and the *Apatosaurus* were remounted in 1998 to show this new understanding.

After discovering *Tyrannosaurus Rex* (1902), Barnum discovered many new dinosaurs and, with the permission of the museum, named many as well, including *Ankylosaurus* (1908), *Kritosaurus* (1910), *Saurolophus* (1911), *Hypacrosaurus* (1913), *Corythosaurus* (1914), *Anchiceratops* (1914), *Leptoceratops* (1914), *Prosaurolophus* (1916), *Dromaeosaurus* (1922), and *Pachycephalosaurus* (1943).

Barnum worked for the American Museum of Natural History as scientist and curator for sixty-six years. If you visit the museum, be sure to look for his name under the many dinosaurs on display there, including *Tyrannosaurus Rex*.

The following museums contain the actual dinosaur fossils from this story:

American Museum of Natural History
79th Street and Central Park West
New York, New York 10025
Tel: 212-313-7278 Web site: www.amnh.org

Carnegie Museum of Natural History
4400 Forbes Avenue
Pittsburgh, Pennsylvania 15213
Tel: 412-622-3131 Web site: www.carnegiemnh.org

Royal Tyrrell Museum
Highway 838 Midland Provincial Park
Drumheller, Alberta, Canada T0J 0Y0
Tel: 888-440-4240 Web site: www.tyrrellmuseum.com

The Academy of Natural Sciences of Philadelphia
1900 Ben Franklin Parkway
Philadelphia, Pennsylvania 19103
Tel: 215-299-1000 Web site: www.acnatsci.org

Yale Peabody Museum
170 Whitney Avenue
New Haven, Connecticut 06511
Tel: 203-432-5050 Web site: www.peabody.yale.edu

Royal Ontario Museum
100 Queen's Park
Toronto, Ontario, Canada ON M5S 2C6
Tel: 416-516-8000 Web site: www.rom.on.ca

Resource Guide (*Books for young readers are marked with an asterisk*)

American Museum of Natural History, 125 Years of Expedition and Discovery, Lyle Rexer and
     Rachel Klein, Harry N. Abrams Publishers in association with the AMNH, 1995.
Bones for Barnum Brown: Adventures of a Dinosaur Hunter, Roland T. Bird, Texas Christian
     University Press, 1985.
Field Guide to Dinosaurs: The Essential Handbook for Travelers in the Mesozoic, Henry Gee and
     Luis V. Rey, Barron's, 2003.
"Field Reports and Barnum Brown's Field Notebooks," The American Museum of Natural History,
     Web site: www.amnh.org.
* *Tyrannosaurus Rex and Barnum Brown*, Brooke Hartzog, Rosen Publishing Group, 1999.
* *The Ultimate Dinosaur Book*, David Lambert, DK Publishing Inc., 1993.
* *What Color Is That Dinosaur?*, Lowell Dingus, Millbrook Press, 1994.
* *The World of Dinosaurs*, Michael Benton, Kingfisher, 2004.

For my parents, Roger and Lois Sheldon,
who always encouraged me to get out there
and explore. —D. S.

First published in the United States of America in 2006 by Walker Publishing Company, Inc.
Distributed to the trade by Holtzbrinck Publishers
For information about permission to reproduce selections from
this book, write to Permissions, Walker & Company,
104 Fifth Avenue, New York, New York 10011

Library of Congress Cataloging-in-Publication Data
Sheldon, David.
Barnum Brown : dinosaur hunter / David Sheldon.
p.   cm.
ISBN-10: 0-8027-9602-8 • ISBN-13: 978-0-8027-9602-8 (hardcover)
ISBN-10: 0-8027-9603-6 • ISBN-13: 978-0-8027-9603-5 (reinforced)
1. Brown, Barnum—Juvenile literature. 2. Paleontologists—United States—
Biography—Juvenile literature. 3. Dinosaurs—Juvenile literature. I. Title.
QE707.B77S54 2006   560.92—dc22   2006000471

The illustrations for this book were created with India ink, gouache,
and acrylic paint on 140-lb. coldpress watercolor paper.
Book design by Donna Mark
Visit Walker & Company's Web site at www.walkeryoungreaders.com
Printed in China

10 9 8 7 6 5 4 3 2 1

All papers used by Walker & Company are natural, recyclable products made
from wood grown in well-managed forests. The manufacturing processes
conform to the environmental regulations of the country of origin.

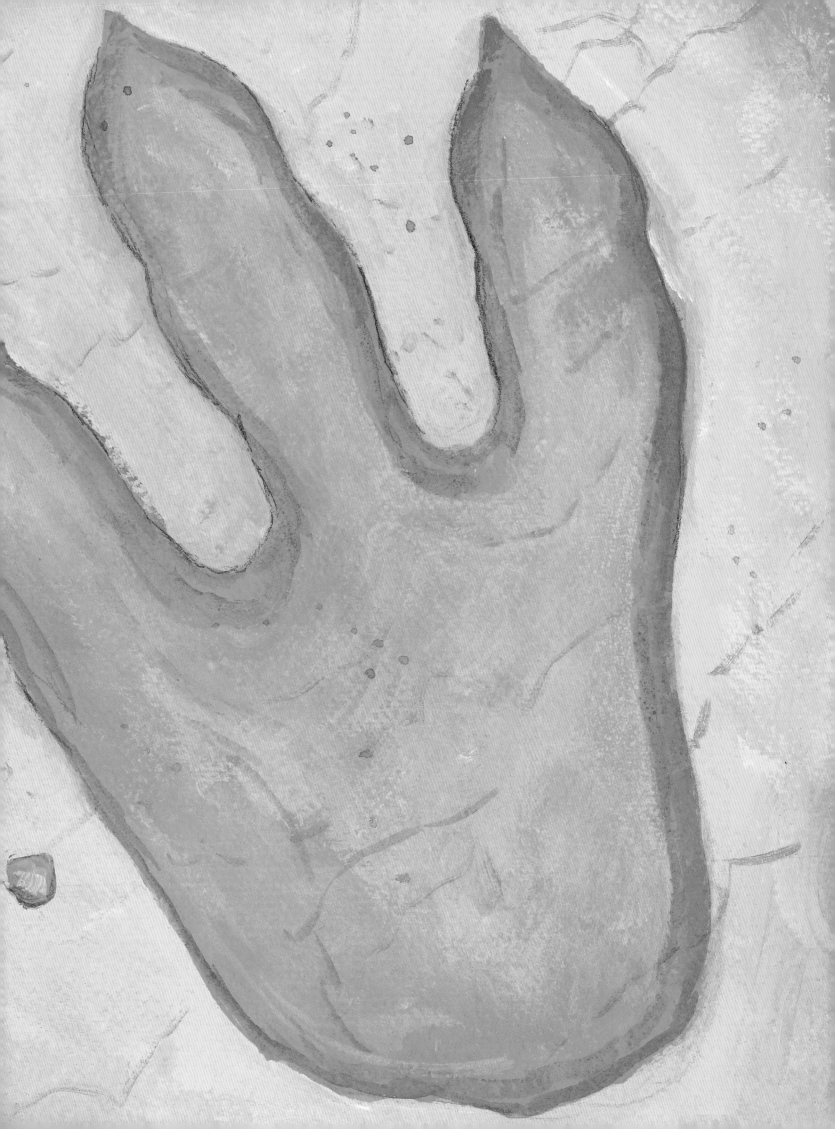

FIELD TRIP 🚌 MYSTERIES

THE
BURGLAR WHO BIT
THE BIG APPLE

by
Steve Brezenoff

r Samantha Archer,

Field Trip Mysteries are published by Stone Arch Books
A Capstone Imprint
151 Good Counsel Drive, P.O. Box 669
Mankato, Minnesota 56002
www.capstonepub.com

Library of Congress Cataloging-in-Publication Data
is available on the Library of Congress website.

Library binding: 978-1-4342-2139-1
Paperback: 978-1-4342-2771-3

I

BIG BURGER

Art Director/Graphic Designer:
Kay Fraser

Summary:
While in New York City on a field trip,
Samantha "Sam" Archer and her friends
find themselves immersed in a run of
crimes at sightseeing locations.

Printed in the United States of America in Stevens Point,
Wisconsin.
022011
006081R

TABLE OF CONTENTS

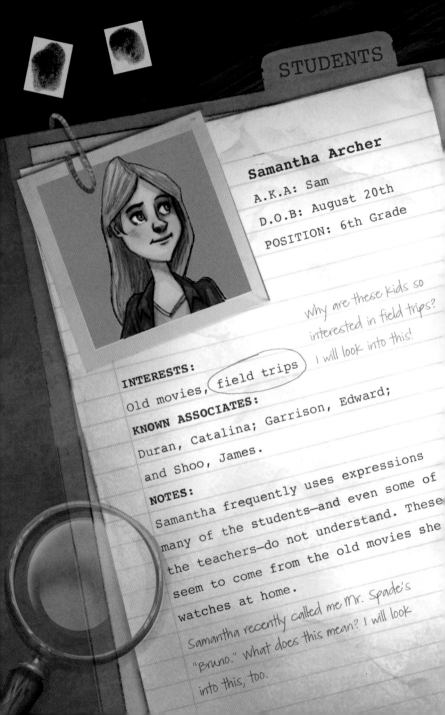

STUDENTS

Samantha Archer

A.K.A: Sam

D.O.B: August 20th

POSITION: 6th Grade

Why are these kids so interested in field trips? I will look into this!

INTERESTS:

Old movies, field trips

KNOWN ASSOCIATES:

Duran, Catalina; Garrison, Edward; and Shoo, James.

NOTES:

Samantha frequently uses expressions many of the students—and even some of the teachers—do not understand. These seem to come from the old movies she watches at home.

Samantha recently called me Mr. Spade's "Bruno." What does this mean? I will look into this, too.

CHAPTER ONE

MY REPORT

This has been a crazy field trip.

Most of my class is asleep. So are the teachers and chaperones. Two days in the Big Apple will make you tired.

And two days in the Big Apple solving the vandalism crime of the century will make you dead tired.

They say there are eight million stories in New York City. And maybe that's so. But this is one of them. It all started when we landed at the airport . . .

* * *

"Everyone over here!" Mr. Spade, our sixth-grade teacher, called. All the students were still making their way off the plane, and the teachers were pushing us along.

"Come on, kids," Ms. Stanwyck, our art teacher, said. "We need to do another head count before we leave the gate."

Cat looked confused. "I don't get it," she said to me. "How could we need another head count now? If the right number of students were on the plane, they must have gotten off."

Gum laughed. "Unless someone jumped off with a parachute," he said.

Egg rolled his eyes. "I think we would have noticed that," he said.

Gum shrugged. "Maybe Anton Gutman locked himself in the bathroom," he said. We all laughed at that. Even Ms. Stanwyck laughed quietly.

The four of us hauled our bags over to where Mr. Spade was standing. The other teachers and chaperones were there too. There was Ms. Duran, Cat's mom; Ms. Stanwyck; Mr. Neff, our science teacher; and Mr. Gutman, Anton's father.

Mr. Neff was pointing at everyone from our class and counting off out loud. "Twenty-two," he said. "That means four are missing. Where are Stan and Puppy and Butter and Candy?"

I tapped Mr. Neff on the shoulder. "Um, Mr. Neff?" I said. "It's Sam, not Stan."

"Yeah," Cat said. "And it's not Puppy. It's Cat."

"And Egg," Egg added.

"And Gum," Gum added.

I nodded and said, "And we're right here. So that makes twenty-six."

Mr. Spade smiled. "Great!" he said. "Let's get to our bus." He turned to Mr. Gutman. "Why don't you and Mr. Neff bring up the rear to make sure we don't have stragglers?" Mr. Spade said.

Anton's dad sighed. "Fine," he said. "Whatever. I'll walk in back with the weird guy."

Cat elbowed me. "Did you hear that?" she whispered. "He's just as rude as his son."

"So that's where Anton gets it," Gum murmured.

Egg already had his camera out. He was snapping some pictures of the airport terminal when we stepped outside.

Then Cat spotted a couple of real New York City cops. "Check it out, Sam!" she said, pointing.

I ran over to them.

"Officers!" I called. I made sure to smile so they would know there was no emergency.

One of them looked at me. He smiled back. "Hey, there, young lady," he said. He was about my height, and he had a thick mustache.

His partner was skinny and way taller than him. "Is everything okay?" he asked me.

"Oh, sure," I said. "I was hoping you'd let my friend take a picture of me with you two."

I turned around and called to Egg. "Hey! Egg! Come over here!" I yelled, waving at him. I stood next to the two cops.

"Of course you can take a picture with us," the shorter policeman said. "Is this your first time in New York City?"

"That's affirmative, officer," I replied. The cops laughed.

Egg had reached us and was snapping some photos. I was about to thank the cops when the walkie-talkie on the shorter policeman's belt started crackling.

"Unit one-twenty reporting," a voice said over the walkie-talkie. "The statue of Ralph Kramden has been robbed at Port Authority Bus Terminal. I repeat, Ralph Kramden's lunchbox is missing."

The two officers looked at each other. "Seriously?" the policeman said. His partner shrugged.

"Sorry, kids," the policeman said. "We have to run." They hurried off.

"What are you kids doing?" a gruff voice said. We spun around.

It was Mr. Gutman. "What do you think would happen if the bus left without you?" he snapped.

"Sorry, Mr. Gutman," I said.

"You could have ruined this trip for me!" Mr. Gutman added. He took me by the wrist and Egg by the camera strap, and dragged us toward the bus. "I wouldn't be able to have fun if everyone was blaming me for two dumb kids going missing at the airport, would I?"

"Um," Egg muttered, "I guess not."

Mr. Gutman brought Egg and me to the bus. "That's the last of them," Mr. Gutman said to the driver.

The door closed with a hiss, and we drove off.

As we came down the airport exit onto the highway, the New York City skyline came into view. Even the grown-ups gasped.

And that's when the adventure really started.

The bus crawled across Manhattan toward our hotel. There were so many people! They were rushing all over the sidewalks, and riding bikes right past our bus and between cars.

On every corner, there was someone selling something, like newspapers or magazines or handbags or food. I could see people selling pretzels and hot dogs and ice cream and gyros and . . . everything you could imagine.

"Wow,"

Gum said.

"I could never live here."

"Why not?" Egg said. "You love trying new foods."

"Exactly!" Gum said. "I'd use up a year's allowance in twenty minutes!"

When the bus finally came to a stop, Cat's mom walked up the aisle to our seats. "Here we are, kids," she said, patting her daughter on the head.

"Mom, I'm not a puppy, remember?" Cat said. "Don't pat my head, please!"

Ms. Duran chuckled. "Okay, sweetie," she said. "Now let's get inside and check out our room."

"I'm not staying in your room," Cat said. "I'm staying with Sam in her room."

"We'll see," Ms. Duran said mysteriously. Then she turned and headed off the bus.

The hotel lobby wasn't what I'd imagined. It was tiny. In fact, it was almost impossible for the whole class to fit in the lobby at the same time. By the time we were all checked in, it was getting late. Mr. Neff and Ms. Stanwyck went out to get pizzas for our dinner. Meanwhile, Cat and I grabbed our key cards to check out our room on the sixth floor.

To my surprise, the room door was wide open. I spotted it from down the hall and grabbed Cat's wrist.

"Wait," I whispered. "Someone's in our room."

Cat's eyes shot open and she stopped. I stepped in front of her and pushed her against the wall of the hallway. Quietly, on tiptoes, I moved along the wall toward our open door.

With my back flat against the wall, I reached the door. In the room, something fell with a thud. Someone muttered under their breath.

Slowly, I bent around the door and peeked into the room. Someone was in the bathroom.

I hissed back to Cat, "Stay there. We have a prowler!"

Still on my toes, I moved into the room without making a sound. I crouched as I walked, moving around the far side of the bathroom door, which was open. The prowler was still in the bathroom. I could hear the sink running.

Then, suddenly, I burst into the bathroom.

"Freeze!" I shouted.

The prowler dropped her toothbrush and shrieked. "Aaaahhh!" she yelled.

"Aaahhh!" I yelled back.

Cat came running into the room. "Mom?" she shouted. "What are you doing in our room?"

CHAPTER THREE

A GIRL

I don't think anyone in my room slept too well that night. Cat had to take the rollaway bed, since she was the shortest. I wouldn't even fit on the thing!

Ms. Duran spent most of the night telling Cat that she couldn't play detective on this field trip. She kept saying how dangerous New York was. Then Cat would roll her eyes. I tried to ignore them.

Ms. Duran fell asleep on one of the beds while Cat and I were still watching TV.

She snores.
Loudly.

Finally morning came. Cat and I got dressed and got out of the room quickly. I think Cat was pretty happy to escape her mom for a while.

In the lobby, Mr. Spade and Mr. Gutman were arguing about something while Mr. Neff and Ms. Stanwyck were handing out packed breakfasts to everyone.

We found Gum and Egg at the front of the group of students waiting for their food.

Mr. Neff did a quick head count. "Everyone's here," he said when Ms. Duran finally made it down to the lobby.

"On the bus," Mr. Spade ordered us. "Our first stop today is the Museum of Natural History."

Anton groaned. "A museum?" he said. "Boooorriiiing."

I'd heard about this museum, and I was excited. "Quiet, Anton," I said.

"Yeah," said Cat. "This museum has dinosaurs and other cool exhibits. I think it's going to be awesome."

"That's because you're a nerd," Anton said. His friends laughed, and the three of them headed to the bus.

We rolled our eyes at one another and followed them.

The American Museum of Natural History was a gorgeous old building, with these big stone steps up the front. They led into a huge marble hall, with a big dinosaur right there to greet you!

When everyone was inside, Mr. Spade shook hands with a woman in a museum uniform.

"Hi, everyone," she said. "I'm Angela. I'll be your guide in the museum today, and in the planetarium after lunch."

Then there was some noise behind us. We all turned around to see what was going on and three older kids — they might have been in high school or even college — came shoving through.

"Excuse us," one of them said. They each held up a card and walked right past the ticket desk into the museum.

"How rude," Cat said. Egg, of course, snapped some photos.

"What was that all about?" I whispered to my friends.

Angela smiled. "Okay, let's start our tour of the museum," she said. Then she turned and began walking into the first hall.

It was so cool. There were dinosaurs and fossils, and a whole exhibit about global warming that Mr. Neff and Cat were excited about.

Right before lunch, Angela took us to the Human Origins hall. It was full of skeletons of prehistoric people. One of the skeletons wasn't labeled.

Egg raised his hand. "Angela?" he said. "Which skeleton is this?"

Angela smiled at him. "Read the plaque on the base of the case," she said.

Egg and I walked around the case looking for the plaque.

All the other cases had a plaque, but this one didn't. At one spot, there was some dried-up glue or tape, like something had been removed.

"This plaque is missing," I called over to Angela. She walked over.

"That's odd," Angela said. "It looks like someone took the plaque off this case. I'd better tell security."

Egg took a photo of the case. Just then, someone pushed past me. I thought it was Anton, but I turned to find a stranger.

It was a girl, about our age, but she wasn't from our class. She was wearing torn jeans and a T-shirt that looked like it was too big for her.

When she realized I was looking at her, the girl turned and pushed herself into the crowd. I lost sight of her.

"Who was that?" I said, elbowing Gum.

"Who was who?" he asked.

"That girl," I said. "The one in the ripped jeans."

Gum looked around. "I didn't see any girl in ripped jeans," he said.

"Weird," I said.

A MISSING PLANET?

After a quick lunch, Angela led us to
the Hayden Planetarium. As we walked, I
spotted the girl in the torn clothes. She was
skulking around near the back of the group.

I grabbed Gum by the wrist to slow him
down. The two of us fell back to the rear of
the group, where Mr. Gutman and Mr. Neff
were walking.

"She's right behind us," I whispered to
Gum.

He turned around. "Who?" he said loudly.

"Shh!" I said. "The girl I told you about. I think she stole that plaque."

Gum nodded. "Gotcha," he said. "On three, we grab her. One. Two."

"Three!" we both said, and we spun around.

The girl jumped, but I had her by the arm. "Who are you?" I asked.

"I . . . ," she said. "I'm in this group, too."

"You are not," Gum said. "We've never seen you before."

The girl looked over my shoulder. "Hey, teacher!" she called out. "These two are bullying me."

I spun, letting go of the girl's arm, and saw Mr. Gutman coming toward me. He looked mad.

"What are you kids doing?" he snapped. "Keep up with the group."

"But, Mr. Gutman," Gum started to say. "This girl —"

But she was gone. Vanished!

"She was right here!" I said to Mr. Gutman.

He shook his head. "Don't care. Keep moving," he said.

Angela clapped, so we all looked at her. "This is our model of the solar system," she said. "If we start at the sun, in the center —"

Egg interrupted her. "Angela," he said, "I think a planet is missing."

"That's right," Angela said. "When this model was made, there was a big surprise: the scientists who made it decided Pluto was not a planet, and they didn't include it. So there are only eight planets on this model."

Egg shook his head. "This model is missing Mercury, too."

Angela looked shocked. She spun around and looked at the model.

"See?" Egg said, pointing at the empty spot. "It should be right here, near the sun."

The whole class, even the teachers and parents, gasped. Angela reached for the walkie-talkie on her hip. "Security," she said. "Security!"

After security came and Gum explained about the planet, we had more sights to see in New York City.

"All right, class," Mr. Spade announced as we gathered outside the planetarium entrance. "Stay together. We're going to wait here for our bus. It's going to take us to the Bronx Zoo."

Everyone in the group was chattering as we stepped into the sunlight outside of the museum. Our bus pulled up, and we got on.

Some people were still excited about the planetarium, and some were excited about getting to the zoo. But not me and my friends. No, the four of us couldn't stop discussing the mysterious girl in the tattered clothes.

"She's behind all this!" I said quietly. "I know shady characters when I see them, and that girl, my friends, is a shady character if I ever saw one."

Gum shook his head and popped a stick of gum (banana) in his mouth. "Sam, Sam, Sam," he said. "There are two Gutmans on this trip, and you're blaming some girl we never heard of? Don't be silly."

Cat rolled her eyes. "Oh, Gum, you're always blaming Anton," she said. "You think he's responsible for everything."

Gum nodded. "I sure do," he said. "Remember that time we found shaving cream in Egg's camera case? I was right that time, wasn't I?"

Egg nodded and said, "How about that time we found Cat's collection of animal figurines in the cafeteria trashcans? That was Anton too."

Cat nodded. "Yeah, it was," she said.

"Okay then," Gum said. "I'm keeping Anton and his dad on my list of suspects for these crimes."

Soon, we reached the zoo. Right at the entrance, a young man was waiting for our group. He was dressed in khaki shorts and a green top.

"Zookeeper," Cat said. "We sure are getting the royal treatment on these tours."

"Yeah," Egg agreed. He lifted his camera. "It's pretty cool, having personal guides at every stop!"

As Egg snapped a shot of the zookeeper, two older boys ran by, practically knocking over Ms. Stanwyck. They each flashed something as they entered the zoo, and they didn't pay any admission fees.

"Just like at the museum," Gum pointed out. "What are they flashing when they run in?"

Mr. Spade stopped to talk to the zookeeper. I looked around. Then I spotted her. The girl from the museum!

"Look," I said quietly to my friends. "There's that girl again."

She was right up by the entrance gate, standing very close to Mr. Spade and the zookeeper.

Mr. Spade turned toward the group. "Okay, everyone come on in," he said. "Our guide, Jeffrey, is going to take us through all the exhibits, starting with the penguins."

Jeffrey waved at us and smiled. "Follow me, kids!" he said.

Just then, the girl in tattered clothes noticed I was watching her. She turned quickly and ran into the zoo.

"Don't run ahead, please," Jeffrey called after her. He started heading after her, but none of the other grown-ups had noticed.

I grabbed Jeffrey by the arm. "She's my friend," I said. "I'll go get her."

The girl dodged around a cotton candy seller, and then around the back of the souvenir stand. I tried to cut her off on the other side, but she was too quick. Before I could grab her, she ducked into the reptile house.

I turned to see where my class was. They were standing around the penguins, and Jeffrey was going on about climates and the difference between penguins and puffins.

I had a few minutes to catch up. My friends would stall our group until I got back. So I ran into the darkness of the reptile house.

It was quiet, and very warm. Once my eyes adjusted to the darkness, I realized there were a few other people inside. I looked carefully, but I didn't see the girl in the tattered clothes.

The reptile house was a long, winding hallway. On both sides were thick windows, separating the viewers from the creatures in the cases. Some of them were lizards, or frogs, and others were huge, deadly snakes.

I moved slowly down the hall, keeping my eyes peeled in the hopes of spotting the mysterious girl. In the low light, I knew she would be easy to miss.

Before long, though, I reached the exit. I'd gone through the whole reptile house, and I hadn't seen her.

Suddenly, there she was. She was in the corner next to the exit, in the darkest spot in the hall, crouched down. Hiding.

"Aha!" I shouted, pointing at her. "You're cornered now."

I lunged for the girl, but she was quick, and got away from me. Her back was to the exit.

"You can't run anymore," I said. "Why don't you just give it up? Give back the plaque from the museum, and the planet from the planetarium!"

She looked at me, confused. Then she spun around and burst through the exit doors.

I was so shocked that I forgot to run. By the time I made it outside, she was gone.

"Darn it," I said under my breath.

My friends walked up. "This just got weirder," Egg said. He then announced loudly, "Jeffrey, look at the big sign over the entrance."

Everyone turned to look.

"Oh no!" Jeffrey said. "The 'Z' is missing from the words Bronx Zoo!"

That night, Gum and Egg hung out in my and Cat's room. Ms. Duran was there, so no one could throw a fit about boys hanging out in a girls' room.

Egg scrolled through his photos. He had a whole bunch of the mysterious girl, plus some of those older kids who had pushed past everyone at the museum and the zoo.

"They're college students," Egg said. "See? They hold up their IDs when they go in."

"Why?" Gum asked. "Do they think anyone cares that they're in college?"

"I saw a sign about that," I explained. "College students with an ID don't have to pay to get in."

"Do you have any pictures of Anton and his dad?" Gum asked.

Egg flipped through the pictures. "Here's one," he said, holding up his camera.

We all looked. It was a shot of the Gutmans near the zoo's exit. Anton and his father had their backs to the camera, and were glancing over their shoulders.

"What are they up to?" I asked. "They look like they're hiding something."

Gum formed a sneaky smile. "Finally," he said, "the evidence we need. Let's go, Egg."

"Where?" Egg asked.

"Down
to our room,"
Gum explained.
"We're going to
confront Anton."

With that, the boys left. We didn't hear anything from them until the next morning.

* * *

Cat and I hurried down to the lobby at seven the next morning. We spotted Anton right away. He and his goonish friends were hanging out near the pay phones, probably making prank calls.

"There you are," I said, walking up to Anton. "So, what do you have to say for yourself?"

Anton looked at me like I was crazy. "Um, how about 'Good morning, dork'?" he said. His friends cracked up.

"I mean about the vandalism," I said. "The stolen planet, and plaque! And the missing 'Z'!"

Anton looked at me like I was a nut, then looked at his friends and said, "Cuckoo! Cuckoo!"

The three of them walked off.

Cat frowned. "Do you think he really didn't know what you were talking about?"

The elevator dinged, and when the doors opened, Egg and Gum stepped off. They both looked tired and depressed.

"Gum!" I called out. Cat and I ran over to them. "What happened last night?" I asked. "Aren't Anton and his dad the culprits?"

Egg shrugged. "We don't know," he said.

"I tried to make Anton talk," Gum said. "We showed him the photo of him and his dad. I really interrogated him. You'd have been proud, Sam."

"I'm sure," I said. "So what did he say?"

"He finally admitted that he and his dad had bought ice cream cones," Gum explained, "and they didn't want to share."

"How rude!" Cat said.

"Let me see that picture again," I said. "I don't believe it!"

Egg flipped through the photos again.

"What's that?" Gum asked, pointing at one photo. "Sam, when did you pose with two cops?"

I laughed. "That was at the airport," I said. "Anton's dad nearly murderized me and Egg for taking so long."

"Aha!" Egg said. "Anton and his dad aren't the ones behind all this! Remember that call the two police officers got, Sam?"

"Great thinking, Egg," I said. "Ralph Kramden's lunchbox — another clear case of tourist attraction vandalism, and it happened when we were still at the airport!"

Egg and I explained about the walkie-talkie call we overheard.

"So if something was stolen at Port Authority, then it couldn't have been the Gutmans," Cat pointed out.

Gum seemed disappointed Anton hadn't been the crook.

Just then, Mr. Neff came up to us. "You kids better get on the bus," he said. "We're off to the Statue of Liberty!"

CHAPTER SEVEN

CAUGHT!

The bus's brakes squealed as we stopped. "Here we are," the driver yelled. "Ferry to the Statue of Liberty and Ellis Island."

Everyone got off, and Mr. Spade and Mr. Gutman guided us through a turnstile toward the ferry dock.

The class walked slowly down a ramp toward the water. As we did, a group of people pushed past us, holding up their student IDs.

"Those people are everywhere!" Cat said.

Egg took more pictures of them. "Hey," he said, taking his camera away from his face. "Look who's here." He pointed down the line. It was the mysterious girl again.

"She won't get away this time," I said. "Once she gets on the boat, there's nowhere to run."

After half an hour or so, the ferry started taking on passengers, including our class and the mysterious girl. The four of us prowled the ship to find her.

It didn't take long. She was sitting near the snack bar, eating a bag of sour cream and onion potato chips.

I walked right up to her and said, "Hey, Cat, do you think that girl paid for those?" I said it loud enough so the girl would hear me.

"Oh, it's you again," the girl said. "Why don't you leave me alone?"

"This is what I do," I said. "Catch snakes and thieves."

"I didn't steal anything!" the girl said. She got to her feet, like she was ready to fight me.

Mr. Spade heard us arguing and came over to us. "What's going on here?" he said. "Are you kids picking on this girl?"

"Mr. Spade," I said, "this is the person responsible for all the vandalism that's been going on."

Mr. Spade scratched his head. He turned to the girl. "Look, I don't know what this is all about, but I do know you're not in my sixth-grade class. Are you alone on this ferry?"

"Why have you been following our class?" Egg asked.

Suddenly, the girl put her face in her hands and started crying. She looked up at me with tears on her cheeks. "I didn't steal anything," she said. "I thought you were chasing me because you knew I wasn't with your group."

"What were you doing?" Mr. Spade asked.

The girl shrugged and looked at her feet. "My mom has to work so much," she explained. "She works all weekend. We never get a chance to do anything fun, like going to museums or to see the Statue of Liberty."

Mr. Spade looked at me, Gum, Egg, and Cat. Then he looked back at the girl. "Is there any way I can get in touch with your mother?" he asked.

"She's at work, like I said," the girl explained. "At the hotel where you're all staying."

"What's your name?" he asked.

"Tilly White," the girl replied.

Mr. Spade got up and took out his cell phone, then walked a few paces away so we couldn't hear him.

I looked at the girl. She was still looking at the floor. "I'm sorry," I said. "I'm sorry I thought you were a crook."

She nodded.

When Mr. Spade came back, he was smiling. "Well, Tilly, looks like it's our lucky day," he said. "I spoke to your mom, and she said we get to hang out with you the rest of the weekend. That is, if you want to, of course."

Finally Tilly looked up. The tears on her cheeks had dried, and she was smiling. "Yes, I do want to," she said.

Mr. Spade added, "Let me know if you need anything, okay?"

Tilly nodded, and Mr. Spade walked off.

She looked at me and my friends. "I'm sorry for ruining your trip," Tilly said.

I waved her off. "Nah," I said. "You just made it more exciting!"

Tilly laughed.

"We still have a case to crack," Gum said. "Maybe Tilly can help."

When the ferry reached Liberty Island, everyone ran to the exit to watch as we pulled up to dock.

And who was up in front? Three older kids, with those student IDs around their necks.

I gathered my three best friends, and our new friend, around me. "Listen," I said. "Since we know the Gutmans aren't the vandals, and since now we know how cool Tilly is . . ."

Tilly smiled at me.

". . . there's really only one more lead we need to follow," I finished.

Gum chewed thoughtfully. "Are you keeping evidence from us?" he said. "Because I didn't think we had any other leads."

"There's one other thing that links all the crimes together," I said.

"Our class?" Cat suggested.

Egg shook his head. "Can't be," he said. "Remember, the lunchbox?"

Tilly nodded. "That's right. Ralph Kramden's lunchbox got stolen!" she said. "I heard about that on the radio. People are pretty mad about it."

"So what's the last clue, Sam?" Gum asked.

"The IDs," I said, crossing my arms. "Let's see your camera, Egg. Do you have any pictures of the other kids we saw with IDs?"

Egg turned on his camera and flipped through the photos. He had quite a few pictures of the college kids.

"Can you zoom in more on the IDs?" I asked.

Egg clicked a couple of buttons and we could see a close-up of the IDs.

"Aha!" I said. "They're all the same color: purple."

"Purple?" Tilly said. "That's New York College's color. They must be students there."

"Then there *is* a connection," Cat said. "All the kids we've seen with IDs must know each other."

"And for some reason," Gum added, "they're all crooks."

The ferry docked. Everyone hurried onto Liberty Island.

The awesome statue loomed over us, holding her famous torch and her book.

"Wow," Egg said, looking up and taking photos. "That's something, huh?"

"I can't believe how big she is," I said.

Anton came up next to me. "Yeah, it's almost as tall as you, beanstalk," he said.

I just rolled my eyes. Then I spotted the kids with IDs.

CHAPTER NINE

THE GAME IS UP

"Let's follow them," I said.

The college kids were hurrying around the statue. We tried not to attract any attention as we went after them. But Ms. Duran spotted us.

"Cat!" she yelled. "Cat, where are you four — I mean, five — going?" She came running over and counted us. "And since when are there five of you?" she asked.

We introduced Tilly, and Cat quickly explained to her mom why we were tailing the college students.

"This sounds dangerous," Cat's mom said. "I'd better tell Mr. Spade what's going on."

Just then, I spied a uniformed policeman walking on the path not far away. "That's all the help we'll need," I said to Ms. Duran.

Then I ran over to the cop. "Hey, flatfoot," I said. "My partners and I are tailing a mob of hoods trying to make off with some hot items, get me?"

The cop tipped his hat back and looked down at me. He was an older man. After his shocked look wore off, he started laughing.

"Well, I haven't heard anyone talk like that since I was about this high," he said, holding his hand at knee level.

"So you're after a bunch of redhots, huh?" the cop said.

I smiled. "You got it," I said. "They've lifted from the last three places we've been, and I think they're also behind the Ralph Kramden lunchbox theft."

The cop looked serious. "I heard about that," he said. "Where'd they get to?"

I pointed to the far side of the statue. "That way, officer," I said. "We better hurry. Who knows what they're planning to do here!"

"You stay way behind me, young lady," the cop said. "These crooks could be dangerous."

Ms. Duran and the others joined me as I followed the policeman. We walked over to the three college kids. They were standing around a copper plaque, and one of them had a crowbar.

"I don't suppose that's going to budge," the cop said. The kids jumped, and the one with the crowbar dropped it. It clanked loudly as it hit the ground.

"What are you doing?" the cop asked.

"N-n-nothing, officer," one of them said.

"You better come with me, and we can talk it over," the cop said, leading them away. "What do you kids know about Ralph Kramden?"

THE LONG GOODBYE

The view from the top of the Statue of Liberty was amazing. But it wasn't as amazing as what happened the next morning.

The policeman I'd met at Liberty Island got the ball rolling, and soon the college kids' stash of stolen goods was found.

It turned out some silly club at New York College was doing an illegal scavenger hunt. Now the city wanted to thank me and my friends for saving some important tourist attractions.

So, with a little time to spare before we had to be at the airport, Mr. Spade took me, Cat, Egg, and Gum to the Port Authority bus station in midtown.

"So that's Ralph Kramden," Gum said, walking up to the statue. "Nice to meet you!"

"He's a character from an old TV show," I explained. "On that show, he drove a bus. That's why the statue is at the bus station."

Cat laughed. "I bet he's glad to have his lunchbox back," she said.

"There you are," Tilly said, walking up to us. "This is pretty cool, huh?"

Some reporters were there, and they took pictures. Egg, of course, took pictures of them right back! All the reporters laughed about that.

Then the mayor came. He gave us each a firm handshake and a special paper thanking us for solving the crime.

Once the excitement had died down, the four of us went over to Tilly.

"Well, Tilly," I said, "it was great to meet you."

"You better email us!" Cat said. I think she was about to start crying.

As we walked off with Mr. Spade to join our classmates and head to the airport, we all waved to Tilly, and she waved back.

"You know what they say," I said to my friends. "If you can make it here, you can make it anywhere."

"And this case is cracked," Gum said. "So I'd say, we made it!"

literary news

MYSTERIOUS WRITER REVEALED!

Steve Brezenoff lives in St. Paul, Minnesota, with his wife, Beth, their son, Sam, and their small, smelly dog, Harry. Besides writing books, he enjoys playing video games, riding his bicycle, and helping middle-school students work on their writing skills. Steve's ideas almost always come to him in his dreams, so he does his best writing in his pajamas.

arts & entertainment

CALIFORNIA ARTIST IS KEY TO SOLVING MYSTERY – POLICE SAY

Early on, C. B. Canga's parents discovered that a piece of paper and some crayons worked wonders in taming the restless dragon. There was no turning back. In 2002 he received his BFA in Illustration from the Academy of Arts University in San Francisco. He works at the Academy of Arts as a drawing instructor. He lives in California with his wife, Robyn, and his three kids.

A Detective's Dictionary

affirmative (uh-FUR-muh-tiv)—giving the answer "yes" or stating that something is true

chaperones (SHAP-ur-onez)—people who watch over other people

emergency (i-MUR-juhn-see)—a sudden and dangerous situation that must be dealt with quickly

interrogated (in-TER-uh-gate-id)—asked many questions

mysterious (miss-TIHR-ee-uhss)—hard to explain or understand

prowler (PROUL-ur)—someone who breaks in to a place

responsible (ri-SPON-suh-buhl)—the cause of something

skulking (SKUHLK-ing)—sneaking around

souvenir (soo-vuh-NIHR)—an object you keep to remind your of a place, a person, or an event

terminal (TUR-muh-nuhl)—a station at either end of a transportation line

vandal (VAN-duhl)—someone who needlessly damages or destroys other people's property

vandalism (VAN-duhl-iz-im)—the destruction of someone else's property

Samantha Archer
Sixth Grade

New York City

A lot of people don't know that New York City used to be called New Amsterdam. But it's true! In fact, when New York City was first inhabited by Europeans, it was a Dutch territory.

It is said that the Dutch explorer Peter Minuet bought the island of Manhattan from the Canarsees, a Native American tribe, for only #65. In 1664, the British renamed the island New York. That was just the beginning of multiculturalism in New York City.

For a long time, immigrants to the United States entered through Ellis Island, located off the southern tip of Manhattan. More than twelve million people entered the U.S. through Ellis Island between 1892 and 1954.

Researchers and family members can look at official documents from the island on the Ellis Island official website, www.ellisisland.org.

Now, people from nearly every country in the world live in New York City. More than 125 different languages are spoken there, and residents of New York come from more than 170 different countries. New York City is a true melting pot!

Samantha: Well done. I have heard that my family came through Ellis Island. I'll have to check out that website.   -Mr. S.

FURTHER INVESTIGATIONS
CASE #FTM05SNY

1. In this book, the whole sixth grade (including me) went on a field trip. What field trips have you gone on? Which one was your favorite, and why?

2. This book takes place in New York City. What do you know about New York? Talk about it.

3. Egg, Gum, Cat, and I thought that Anton had committed the crimes. Why do you think we thought that?

IN YOUR OWN DETECTIVE'S NOTEBOOK . . .

1. Pretend you're Tilly. Write a letter to me and my friends about what you've been doing since our field trip.

2. Gum, Egg, Cat, and I are best friends. Write about your best friend. Don't forget to include what you like about your friend.

3. This book is a mystery story. Write your own mystery story!

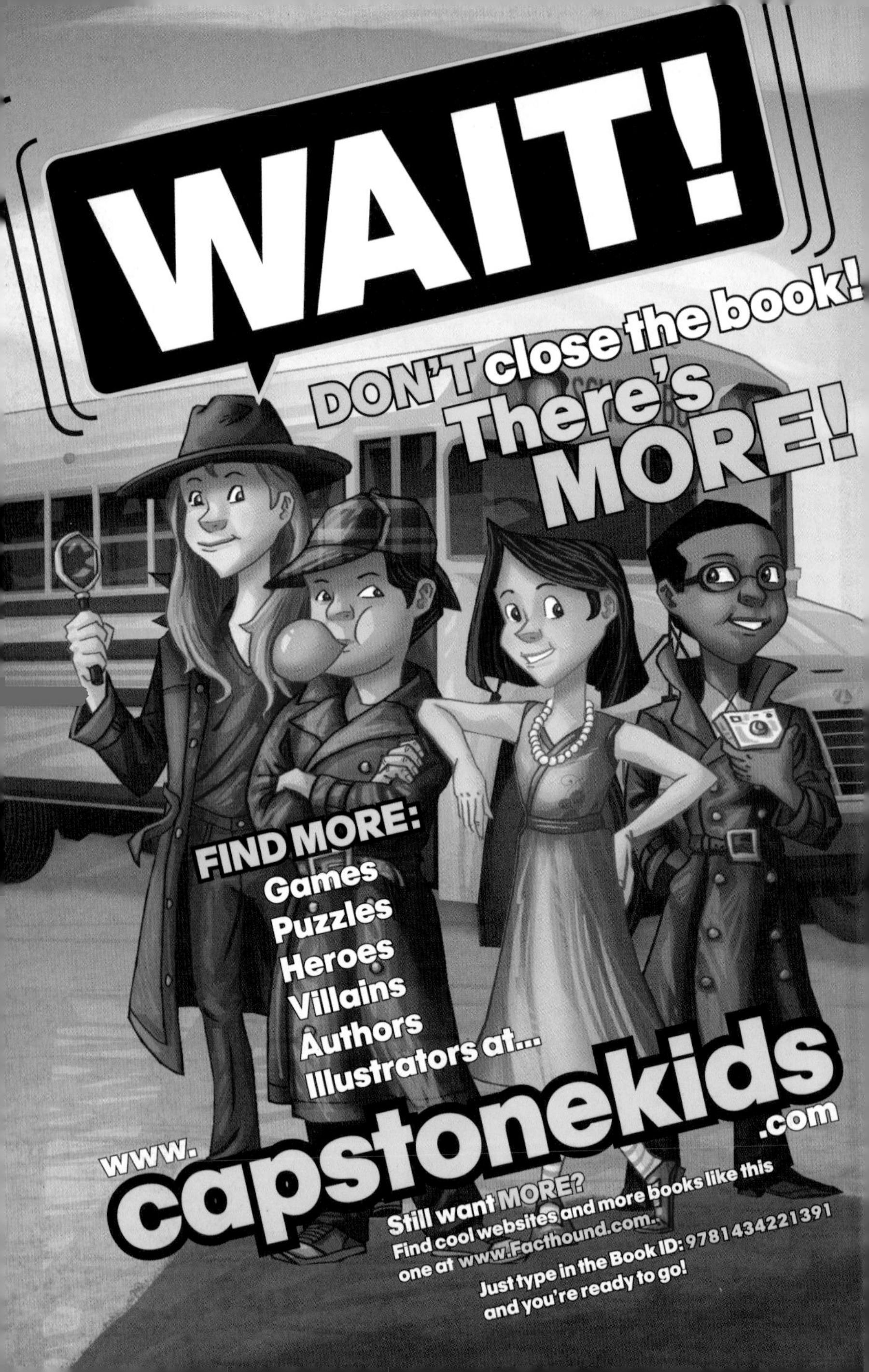